BATTLE OF THE GODDESSES

DIANA
VS
ATHENA

by Lydia Lukidis

CAPSTONE PRESS
a capstone imprint

Published by Capstone Press, an imprint of Capstone
1710 Roe Crest Drive, North Mankato, Minnesota 56003
capstonepub.com

Library of Congress Cataloging-in-Publication Data is available
on the Library of Congress website
ISBN: 9781666343649 (hardcover)
ISBN: 9781666343663 (paperback)
ISBN: 9781666343670 (ebook PDF)

Summary: It's a battle of the hunter versus the warrior! Roman goddess
Diana reigns over nature, fertility, childbirth, and the boundary
between Earth and the underworld. The Greek goddess Athena is
known for her wisdom and courage in battle. If these two goddesses
were to go head-to-head, who would come out on top?

Editorial Credits
Editor: Julie Gassman; Designer: Heidi Thompson; Media Researchers:
Jo Miller and Pam Mitsakos; Production Specialist: Tori Abraham

Image Credits
Alamy: Album, 7, 11, Chronicle, 21, History and Art Collection, 6;
Getty Images/Hemera Technologies, 9; Newscom: Album/Prisma,
19; Shutterstock: Anastasiya A_S_I_D, 12, Anna Krivitskaya, 4, 28,
Babin, Cover (Top), delcarmat, 25, DesignRage, 27 (Left), German
Vizulis, 5, 29, Herbstkind, 23, Katerina Kreker, 22, KUCO, 17, Mihail
Siergiejevicz, 27 (Right), Oliver Denker, 15, Zyankarlo, Cover (Bottom)

All internet sites appearing in back matter were available and accurate
when this book was sent to press.

Printed and bound in the USA. PO4882

TABLE OF CONTENTS

Words in **bold** are in the glossary.

THE HUNTER VS. THE WARRIOR

Diana's reddish-brown hair sparkles in the sunlight. The Roman goddess hikes through the forest as a herd of deer follows her. She stops to pet them. A wild and free-spirited goddess, Diana roams the woods every day.

Diana adores animals, nature, and hunting. She's also the goddess of **fertility** and childbirth. Plus, she's in charge of part of the **underworld**.

Diana

FACT

Diana is from the Roman religion. But she's connected to the Greek goddess Artemis. They are very similar.

Now check out the Greek goddess Athena's list of qualities. Popular? Check. One of the 12 **Olympians**? Check. Fierce warrior and goddess of wisdom? Check and check.

Athena is in charge of many things, from defending towns to arts and crafts. No wonder she stars in so many Greek **myths**. Not to mention she's Zeus's favorite child.

Athena

Which goddess do you think is more powerful? You'll have to read more about Diana and Athena as they battle it out. The duel is on!

HOW DID THEY GET HERE?

Diana's origin myth is full of drama. Let's start with the basics. Her dad is the god Jupiter. He married the goddess Juno. Here's a wild fact: Jupiter and Juno are brother and sister. But the drama doesn't end there. Juno isn't Diana's mother! Diana's father had a mistress named Latona.

Jupiter and Juno were the children of Saturn and Ops.

Latona is the goddess of motherhood.

Juno found out her husband was having a child with Latona. She flew into a jealous rage. She didn't allow Latona to give birth anywhere on land. Instead, she sent her to the floating island of Delos.

Soon after, Latona gave birth to the twin gods Diana and Apollo. Diana was born easily. Meanwhile, it took nine days and nine nights before Apollo was born. Even though Diana was a few days old, she helped her mother give birth to Apollo.

If you think Diana's origin myth is shocking, wait until you hear Athena's story. Zeus, the main ruler of all Greek gods, is her dad. Her mom is the goddess Metis, Zeus's first wife. One day, Metis became pregnant with Athena. That's when things took a strange turn.

Zeus heard a **prophecy** that his wife's child may overthrow him. Not one to be outdone, Zeus had to act fast. He decided to do the unthinkable. He *swallowed* up Metis in one gulp, baby and all.

Soon after, Zeus had some royal headaches. He asked the god Hephaestus to whack him on the head with an ax for relief. Then, poof! Athena sprang forth fully grown. She was in full armor. She belted out a mighty war chant.

Zeus is the god of the sky and thunder.

SUPER STRENGTHS

What are Diana's strengths? For one, she's a superstar **midwife**. She helps women become pregnant. Then she looks after them during childbirth.

Diana is popular. Women from all over the world used to seek her help. They worshipped her as a fertility goddess. They even left candles in earthen pots in the shape of babies and **wombs** at her shrine near Rome.

Wonder Woman!

Did you know Diana inspired the fictional character of Wonder Woman? Her **civilian** name is Diana Prince, and her Amazon identity is Princess Diana of Themyscira. Like the goddess Diana, Wonder Woman is smart and independent. She's just as powerful and fights a fierce battle.

Diana not only protected mothers and children. She also protected those from poorer classes, such as enslaved people. When enslaved people entered her temple, they were safe. Today, many people celebrate Nemoralia. It is also known as the Festival of Torches. This Roman festival begins on August 13. It honors Diana and the poorer classes.

Women performed a special dance in honor of Diana.

In some myths, an owl helped Athena see all sides of a problem, so she could see the truth.

Athena is ready for the duel with strengths of her own. First off, she's one smart cookie. Gods and goddesses come to her for advice all the time. Sporting the owl as her symbol, Athena is known for her wisdom, and so are owls.

She once had a massive blowout with Poseidon, god of the seas. The fight was over who would represent the city of Athens. Athena outsmarted Poseidon.

Here's how it went down. They both had to give the city a gift. Poseidon used his muscles. He struck his **trident** into a rock and a saltwater spring erupted. But Athena used her brain instead. She planted an olive tree. Victory! She won the contest because her tree was more useful. It gave the Athenians fruit, oil, and wood.

Ready, set, aim! Master of the bow and arrow, Diana is a highly skilled archer with perfect aim. Make no mistake, she's one of the greatest hunters in ancient Rome. She's also an expert at tracking animals.

Virgil and Horace, famous ancient Roman poets, wrote about Diana's ability to cast magic spells. This comes in handy because she guards the boundary between Earth and the underworld. She helps people travel from one world to another. Diana is a symbol for any crossroads. For example, sometimes a hunter finds himself in a forest late at night. Diana can help him decide which way to go.

FACT

Diana has many other strengths. In fact, people worship her as a triple goddess. That includes goddess of the hunt, goddess of the moon, and goddess of the underworld.

Diana preferred to spend her time with animals rather than
people or gods.

While Diana is a skilled hunter, Athena is a fierce warrior. In the war of Zeus against the giants, she advised her father and Heracles. She didn't sit on the sidelines though. She fought in the war herself. She is one of the strongest goddesses. She once loaned a **mortal** prince some of her strength. He struck Ares, the god of war, so hard that it nearly killed him.

Athena also helps many heroes. For example, she helped Perseus kill the monster Medusa. Athena knew that if Perseus looked directly at the monster, he would turn to stone. She helped by giving him a polished shield. That way, Perseus looked at Medusa's reflection as he hunted her down.

FACT

Athena has many other strengths. She's the goddess of courage, mathematics, and strategy. Even though she's the goddess of war, she's also a peacemaker. She isn't into senseless violence.

Perseus (left) was considered a hero for killing Medusa (right).

AWESOME SUPERPOWERS

Diana and Athena are both **immortal** goddesses. But they possess different powers. Diana starts off strong with her animal superpowers. As goddess of the woods, she can talk to animals. She can also control their movements and behavior. She can even turn herself or humans into animals!

For example, the Roman poet Ovid wrote about a famous Diana myth. Actaeon, a talented hunter, was once hunting deer in the woods. The hunt was going well. As the sun's rays sizzled, Actaeon found a water spring and used it to cool off. Then, surprise! Diana was bathing there—naked. She was embarrassed. She grabbed her bow and splashed Actaeon with water. He instantly sprouted horns and turned into a deer.

Actaeon (left) was killed by his hounds after Diana turned
him into a deer.

Athena also has some awesome powers. First off, she can physically transform herself. For example, she changed herself into Odysseus's old friend Mentes in the famous Greek poem *The Odyssey.*

Athena is also a master inventor. She invented useful items such as the chariot, plow, and rake. Some of these things are handy for people working in the fields. At the beginning of spring, farmers offer her thanks. They're grateful for the protection she sends to their land and crops.

Helping Hercules

Athena often uses her superpowers to help heroes. For example, she helped the god Hercules during his 12 labors. According to the famous myth, he had 12 important missions. In one mission, he had to scare off the Stymphalian birds. They were terrorizing everyone in the area. Athena used her powers to create a loud noise that scared off the birds.

Athena is also super crafty and invented weaving and pottery. In fact, people call her the greatest weaver in Greek mythology. And her talents don't end there. She's also musical and invented the flute.

Athena was known for her weaving.

Both goddesses are independent and strong-willed. Diana is all about girl power and does her own thing. She loves helping women any way she can. She's not interested in finding a husband. As the goddess of purity, she remains unmarried. A lover of nature, Diana usually has a peaceful spirit. But make no mistake, if trouble arises, she will fight at a moment's notice.

Diana

Athena is also all about girl power. She values wisdom and is ready to stand up for what's right no matter what. She's brave enough to take on **titans**, other gods, and monsters. Like Diana, she doesn't want a husband and remains unmarried.

Athena

GODDESS ISSUES

Sure, both goddesses are powerful. But they aren't perfect. Diana can be unpredictable. She's connected to the moon, which changes all the time, just like her. She can also be quick-tempered and arrogant.

Worse yet, Diana has an even darker side while in the underworld. She can be unforgiving and bloodthirsty. In fact, she can be downright evil. She sometimes practices witchcraft and evil charms. And though she mainly uses her bow and arrow for hunting, she sometimes uses them on mortals when they anger her.

Diana did not approve of most mortal men and sometimes turned her weapon on them.

Athena also has issues. First off, she's a full-on drama queen. In one myth, she blinded Tiresias just because he saw her in the shower. Not only that, she can hold a mean grudge.

Look at what happened to poor Arachne. Arachne was a mortal craftswoman. One day, she dared boast she was better at weaving than Athena. Athena demanded she take it back. Arachne refused. Fueled by rage, Athena challenged her to a weaving contest. But Athena didn't like what Arachne was weaving. She tore the fabric to shreds and turned Arachne into a giant spider.

Athena also has a bad temper. You don't want to get on her bad side. Just ask Medusa. She used to be a beautiful young woman. But then Athena turned her into a horrible monster with snakes for hair just because she dated the wrong god.

Both Diana and Athena have strengths, powers, and weaknesses. Considering everything you just learned, who do *you* think is the greater goddess?

Athena

Diana

DIANA VS. ATHENA AT A GLANCE

Name:	Diana
Goddess of:	Wild animals, nature, hunting, fertility, moon, childbirth, the boundary between Earth and the underworld
Appearance:	Diana is tall, beautiful, and athletic, with reddish-brown hair. She wears a short tunic (to hunt easily) and a cloak with a belt that has a jeweled clasp.
Weapons:	A bow and golden arrows
Strengths:	Protects mothers, children, and enslaved people, master of the bow and arrow, great hunter, can guide people to the underworld
Powers and abilities:	Can talk to and control animals, turns humans into animals, is very independent
Weaknesses:	She has an unpredictable nature and can be vengeful, quick-tempered, and arrogant.
Symbol:	Accompanied either by a deer or hunting dogs

Name:	Athena
Goddess of:	Wisdom and good advice, war and the defense of towns, purity, courage, and crafts
Appearance:	Athena is tall and thin, with dark brown hair. She wears a long robe, a crested golden helmet, and body armor.
Weapons:	A spear and a shield called the **aegis**, featuring an image of Medusa's head
Strengths:	Smart, wise, fierce warrior, strong, courageous, peacemaker, stands for morality, helps heroes
Powers and abilities:	Master inventor, helps with farming, great abilities with weaving and pottery, can shape-shift into other forms
Weaknesses:	She has a bad temper, holds a grudge, and can be self-centered.
Symbol:	Owl

GLOSSARY

aegis (EE-jis)—Athena's shield with a picture of Medusa's head

civilian (si-VIL-yuhn)—a regular person who's not part of the army or the police force

fertility (fer-TIL-i-tee)—the ability to become pregnant

immortal (i-MOR-tuhl)—living forever and never dying

midwife (MID-wife)—a person trained to help women give birth

mortal (MOR-tuhl)—a human who will eventually die

myth (MITH)—a story from ancient times; myths often tried to explain natural events

Olympians (uh-LIM-pee-uhns)—the 12 Olympians were the main gods and goddesses in Greek mythology

prophecy (PROF-uh-see)—a prediction about the future

titans (TYE-tuhns)—ancient and original family of gods before the Olympians

trident (TRY-dent)—a long spear with three sharp points at its end

underworld (UHN-dur-wurld)—the mythical land of the dead

womb (WOOM)—the organ in females where the young develop before birth

READ MORE

Chae, Yung In. *Goddess Power: 10 Empowering Tales of Legendary Women.* Emeryville, CA: Rockridge Press, 2020.

Greenberg, Imogen. *Athena: Goddess of Wisdom and War.* New York: Amulet Books, 2021.

Leavitt, Amie Jane. *Diana: Roman Goddess of the Hunt.* North Mankato, MN: Capstone, 2020.

INTERNET SITES

Diana the Huntress, Roman Goddess: Importance & Mythology study.com/academy/lesson/dianna-the-huntress-roman-goddess-importance-mythology.html

Greek Gods: Athena historyforkids.net/ancient-greek-gods.html#Athena

Greek Mythology: Athena ducksters.com/history/ancient_greece/athena.php

INDEX

ABOUT THE AUTHOR

Lydia Lukidis is a lover of science, the ocean, and Greek mythology. She's also the author of more than 35 trade and educational books for children, as well as 30 ebooks. Her STEM title, *The Broken Bees' Nest* (Kane Press, 2019), was nominated for a CYBILS Award. Lydia is passionate about fostering a love for literacy with children and offers writing workshops and author visits in elementary schools.